YOSEMITE NATIONAL PARK, CALIFORNIA

THIS BOOK BELONGS TO

13-Digit ISBN: 978-1604336412
10-Digit ISBN: 1604336412

This book may be ordered by mail from the publisher. Please include $3.95 for postage and handling. Please support your local bookseller first!

Books published by Cider Mill Press Book Publishers are available at special discounts for bulk purchases in the United States by corporations, institutions, and other organizations. For more information, please contact the publisher.

Cider Mill Press Book Publishers
"Where good books are ready for press"
12 Spring Street | PO Box 454
Kennebunkport, Maine 04046
Visit us on the Web! www.cidermillpress.com

Typography: Georgia, Colonna MT, Type Embellishments One LET

Image credits, in order of appearance:
Cover wrap image: courtesy of Bruce Wolfe; front endpapers: Nevada Fall along John Muir Trail, Yosemite National Park (Robert Ciccetti/shutterstock.com) and John Muir, photographed by Edward Hughes, c. 1902 (Library of Congress, LC-DIG-ppmsca-18938); pen illustration on page v: researcher97/Shutterstock.com; border illustration in the introduction: hoverfly/Shutterstock.com; John Muir, c. 1902 (Library of Congress, cph 3b00011); Yosemite's Domes, photographed by Carleton E. Watkins, c. 1865 (Library of Congress, ppmsca 09984); El Capitan, published in *Our National Parks*, 1909 (Internet Archive); John Muir (Library of Congress, ggbain 06861); John Muir with walking stick, 1906 (Wikimedia Commons); Merced River and Vernal Fall, Yosemite, published in *Our National Parks*, 1909 (Internet Archive); Yosemite Valley, photographed by Carleton E. Watkins, c. 1865 (Library of Congress, ppmsca 09983); Muir Glacier, Alaska, 1902 (Library of Congress, cph 3c36267); Grand Canyon from the head of the Grand View Trail, Arizona, 1906 (Library of Congress, LC-D4-19248); John Muir, c. 1911 (Internet Archive); Theodore Roosevelt and John Muir on Glacier Point, Yosemite National Park, 1903 (Library of Congress, ppmsca 36413); back endpapers: John Muir, c. 1870, published in *A Thousand-Mile Walk to the Gulf*, 1916 (Internet Archive) and John Muir House in Martinez, California (Library of Congress, HABS CAL,7-MART,1-)

Printed in China
2 3 4 5 6 7 8 9 0

JOHN MUIR

SIGNATURE
NOTEBOOK

CIDER MILL
PRESS

BOOK
PUBLISHERS

KENNEBUNKPORT, MAINE

Introduction

BY J. SCOTT DONAHUE, *SIERRA* MAGAZINE CONTRIBUTOR
AND AUTHOR OF *50 WAYS TO SAVE THE HONEY BEES
(AND CHANGE THE WORLD)*

*The mountains are calling.
Do you hear them?*

For John Muir—prolific botanist, bold mountaineer, and steadfast conservationist—the mountains called to him endlessly. And he answered the only way he could: by taking bold, tireless steps toward the great wide open and writing about the wonder of it all.

Born in 1838, John Muir was only a ten-year-old sapling when he, his mother, father, and six siblings immigrated to the United States from Scotland. The Muirs immediately took to farming in rural Wisconsin, instilling in their children a devout practice of Calvinism. Under his father's zealous discipline and homeschooling, John Muir endured cruel and punitive lessons. Understandably, this steered him away from a Calvinist understanding of God; Muir instead found God, along with refuge and solitude, in the pastoral land to which he escaped. In a way, Muir built his own fundamentalist faith that was devoted to the pristine, natural world.

Leaving behind the strictures of his home, Muir took up study at the University of Wisconsin. His stint as a student lasted three years before he left for Ontario to be among the boreal forests; he would later refer to this tenure as the "University of Wilderness." A bit of a Renaissance man, he wandered a great deal from vocation to vocation, invention to invention, factory to factory. He came of age in the thick, tumultuous smoke of the Industrial Revolution and Manifest Destiny, and filled notebooks with botany sketches, field notes, and ecstatic musings. In order to support his wanderlust, Muir contributed to technological advancements in industry. He invented lathing machines, drew plans for a self-setting sawmill (an elaborate, counter-weighted buzz saw), and continuously pushed the boundaries of his creativity.

Then it all went black. A file he was using to fix machinery flew into his eye, which immediately went blind, and shortly after, the other eye went blind, too. The accident nearly cost the twenty-nine-year-old inventor his sight. For six weeks, he sat with bandages over his eyes, in complete darkness (doctor's orders). It was in those weeks of boredom, solitude, and blindness that the young Muir took hundreds of imaginary trips to Yosemite Valley. In the vastness of his imagination, he conjured images of Bridalveil Fall, Half Dome, Sentinel Dome, and the commanding nose of El Capitan: places he had read about, but never seen.

The return of his sight awoke something in Muir, and he left the factory for a lifetime in the forest. From Indianapolis to Florida's Gulf of Mexico, he walked over 1,000 miles, taking field notes as he went. At times, the man had only a bread crust, bundle of tea, and a Ralph Waldo Emerson book to tide him over. In 1868, Muir traveled to San Francisco, where he lasted only one day before asking a passerby carrying carpentry tools the nearest way out of town. "Where do you wish to go?" the carpenter asked. "Anyplace that is wild," answered Muir.

Upon arriving in Yosemite in the winter of 1868, John Muir found the wild he was looking for. He later recalled thinking, as he saw the valley unfold its glaciated canyons and white-granite pinnacles, "Oh no, not for me." This humility characterized his reverence for Wilderness (with a capital "W"). Filling his notebooks with notes and sketches, he made fine discoveries in naturalism. He was the first to note that ancient glaciers had, over thousands of years, carved the valley and smoothed the granite walls.

Such glaciated granite spurred Muir to explore every corner of the High Sierra. He was the first recorded man to sink an ice ax into several Sierra Nevada summits, notably Mount Ritter, Cathedral Peak, and Mount Whitney's Mountaineer's Route. It was during these honeymoon years in Yosemite that he finally met his longtime travel "companion" and literary influence, Emerson, whom Muir described as "the most serene, majestic, sequoia-like soul" he had ever encountered. Muir shared Emerson's transcendentalist belief in a common bond between the soul and wild nature.

Nature required control, at least according to the then-common belief related to America's progress across the West. In the years when Muir trekked back and forth between his log cabin near Yosemite Falls to his growing family and farm in Martinez, California, he became increasingly wary of such "progress," often said sardonically. He witnessed such unrestrained "progress" in the form of felled sequoia trees, meadows ravaged by sheep flocks, and mighty rivers destroyed by man-made dams. So in 1873, Muir left Yosemite at once for his desk, from which he would write his most fiery letters and essays calling for conservation.

For ten months, Muir lived in self-described "exile" while his ice ax collected dust. From his home study, he penned his greatest works: polemics to politicians, and essays and editorials for newspapers and science journals decrying the fate of Yosemite to logging, overgrazing, and greed.

Even in his forties and fifties, the spry John Muir worked most prolifically. He published books about his travels to Alaska and the Pacific Northwest, and about cofounding the Sierra Club—all while raising two daughters and maintaining a farm with wife, Louie Strentzel Muir. Eventually, Muir's activism caught the attention of rough-riding President Theodore Roosevelt. The two took a legendary trip in 1903; camping atop Yosemite's Glacier Point and sipping coffee from tin mugs, they came up with a plan to save the valley and other wondrous slices of the country.

The legacy of John Muir—writer, visionary conservationist, and scientist—began with a notebook. This legacy can be seen in every national park, monument, and protected piece of wilderness. The mountains, rivers, oceans, deserts, and plains are calling. What do they say to *you*?

IN EVERY
WALK WITH NATURE
ONE RECEIVES
FAR MORE THAN
HE SEEKS.

—*Steep Trails* (1918)

John Muir, c. 1902

Yosemite's Domes, 1865

ANOTHER GLORIOUS DAY,
THE AIR AS
DELICIOUS
TO THE LUNGS
**AS NECTAR TO
THE TONGUE.**

—*My First Summer in the Sierra* (1911)

WE CANNOT FORGET ANYTHING.

MEMORIES MAY ESCAPE
THE ACTION OF WILL,
MAY SLEEP A LONG TIME,
BUT WHEN
**STIRRED BY THE
RIGHT INFLUENCE,**
THOUGH THAT INFLUENCE
BE LIGHT AS A SHADOW,
THEY FLASH INTO
FULL STATURE
AND LIFE
WITH EVERYTHING IN PLACE.

—*A Thousand-Mile Walk to the Gulf* (1916)

NATURE IS EVER AT WORK
BUILDING AND PULLING DOWN,
**CREATING AND
DESTROYING,**
KEEPING EVERYTHING
WHIRLING
AND FLOWING,
ALLOWING NO REST
BUT IN RHYTHMICAL MOTION,
CHASING
EVERYTHING
IN ENDLESS SONG
OUT OF ONE BEAUTIFUL FORM
INTO ANOTHER.

—*Our National Parks* (1901)

WHEN WE CONTEMPLATE
**THE WHOLE GLOBE
AS ONE GREAT**
DEWDROP,
STRIPED AND DOTTED WITH
CONTINENTS AND ISLANDS,
FLYING THROUGH SPACE
WITH OTHER STARS
**ALL SINGING
AND SHINING
TOGETHER AS ONE,**
THE WHOLE UNIVERSE
APPEARS AS AN
INFINITE STORM
OF BEAUTY.

—*Travels in Alaska* (1915)

John Muir with sequoia tree

WHEREVER YOU CHANCE TO BE
ALWAYS SEEMS AT THE MOMENT
OF ALL PLACES THE BEST;
AND YOU FEEL THAT

THERE CAN BE NO
HAPPINESS
IN THIS WORLD,
OR IN ANY OTHER,
FOR THOSE WHO MAY
NOT BE HAPPY HERE.

—*Travels in Alaska* (1915)

CLIMB THE MOUNTAINS
AND GET THEIR GOOD TIDINGS.

NATURE'S PEACE

**WILL FLOW INTO YOU
AS SUNSHINE
FLOWS INTO TREES.**

THE WINDS WILL BLOW THEIR
OWN FRESHNESS INTO YOU,
AND THE STORMS THEIR ENERGY,
WHILE CARES WILL
DROP OFF LIKE
AUTUMN LEAVES.

—*Our National Parks* (1901)

I GAVE HEED TO
THE CONFIDING
STREAM,
MINGLED FREELY WITH THE
**THE FLOWERS
AND LIGHT,**
AND SHARED IN THE
CONFIDENCE OF THEIR
EXCEEDING
PEACE.

—"By-Ways of Yosemite Travel" (1874)

Merced River and Vernal Fall, Yosemite National Park

WHEN A MAN PLANTS A TREE
HE PLANTS HIMSELF.
EVERY ROOT
IS AN ANCHOR,
OVER WHICH HE RESTS
WITH GRATEFUL INTEREST,
AND BECOMES
SUFFICIENTLY CALM
TO FEEL THE JOY OF
LIVING.

—*Steep Trails* (1918)

Yosemite Valley, c. 1865

WHEN I HEARD THE STORM
I MADE HASTE TO JOIN IT; FOR
IN STORMS
NATURE HAS
ALWAYS SOMETHING
EXTRA FINE
TO SHOW US.

—"An Adventure with a Dog and a Glacier" (1897)

Muir Glacier, Alaska, 1902

THE WHOLE MOUNTAIN
APPEARED AS ONE
GLORIOUS
MANIFESTATION
OF DIVINE POWER,
ENTHUSIASTIC
AND BENEVOLENT,
GLOWING
LIKE A COUNTENANCE WITH
INEFFABLE REPOSE
AND BEAUTY
BEFORE WHICH WE COULD ONLY
GAZE IN DEVOUT AND LOWLY
ADMIRATION.

—*Steep Trails* (1918)

THE WARM, BROODING DAYS ARE
FULL OF LIFE
AND THOUGHTS
OF LIFE TO COME,
RIPENING SEEDS WITH
NEXT SUMMER IN THEM OR
A HUNDRED
SUMMERS.

—*Our National Parks* (1901)

Grand Canyon from the head of the Grand View Trail, Arizona, 1906

I WISH I COULD BE MORE
MODERATE IN MY DESIRES,
BUT I CANNOT, AND
**SO THERE IS
NO REST.**

—*Letters to a Friend* (1915)

NO OTHER TREE

IN THE WORLD,
AS FAR AS I KNOW, HAS

LOOKED DOWN
ON SO MANY
CENTURIES AS THE

SEQUOIA,

OR OPENS SUCH IMPRESSIVE AND
SUGGESTIVE VIEWS INTO HISTORY.

—*The Mountains of California* (1894)

John Muir with sequoia tree, c. 1911

ONE TOUCH OF NATURE MAKES
THE WHOLE WORLD
KIN.

—*Our National Parks* (1901)

About Cider Mill Press Book Publishers

Good ideas ripen with time. From seed to harvest, Cider Mill Press brings fine reading, information, and entertainment together between the covers of its creatively crafted books. Our Cider Mill bears fruit twice a year, publishing a new crop of titles each spring and fall.

Visit us on the web at

www.cidermillpress.com

or write to us at

12 Spring Street

PO Box 454

Kennebunkport, Maine 04046

JOHN MUIR HOUSE, ALHAMBRA BOULEVARD